Aristotle

Born in 384 BC within twenty years of the deaths of
Sophocles, Euripides and Socrates, Aristotle was son of
the royal physician to King Philip of Macedonia. His
parents died when he was young, and at 17 he went to
Athens to study under Plato. After twenty years at the
Academy, ended by Plato's death in 347, Aristotle spent
some years as a travelling professor. He set up his own
Academy at Assos in Asia Minor, which was also where
he got married. He moved on to Lesbos and then
became tutor to the young Alexander the Great at the
Macedonian Court at Pella. In 335, aged 49, he returned
to Athens, then the intellectual capital of the world, and
established his own teaching institution, the Lyceum.
Research students came from all over the Greek world
to work on projects which Aristotle directed. With
Alexander's death in 323, Aristotle retired to Chalcis,
where he died within the year. His Lyceum survived for
almost a thousand years.

Kenneth McLeish

Born in 1940, McLeish was a schoolmaster before
turning full-time to writing and translating. As well as
most of the surviving plays from Ancient Greece, he has
translated work by, among others, Feydeau, Ibsen, Jarry,
Labiche, Molière and Strindberg. His books cover a
wide range of subjects with music and literature
figuring large. He died in 1997.

Aristotle

*P*oetics

translated and introduced by
Kenneth McLeish

THEATRE COMMUNICATIONS GROUP
New York

Translation and introduction copyright
© 1998 by Kenneth McLeish

Poetics is published by Theatre Communications Group,
355 Lexington Avenue, New York, NY 19917.

This edition is published in an arrangement with
Nick Hern Books.

A CIP catalog record for this book is available on file
at the Library of Congress.

ISBN 1-55936-170-0

First U.S. edition, March 1999

Typeset in Bitstream Aldine by Country Setting,
Kingsdown, Kent CT14 8ES

Printed and bound in Great Britain by Cox & Wyman,
Reading, Berks

Contents

4/23/02

$87 96

Introduction

Aristotle (384-322BC)

Aristotle was a Macedonian, son of the royal physician to King Philip. He studied with Plato in Athens, and after Plato's death spent some years as a travelling professor. (Among other things, he tutored the Macedonian prince Alexander, the future Alexander the Great.) In 335, aged 49, he set up a teaching institution of his own in Athens; it survived for almost a millennium, one of the longest-lasting 'universities' of the ancient world.

Like most other intellectuals of the time – the Greek word 'philosopher' means no more than 'lover of knowledge' – Aristotle held that nothing lay outside his interest or the scope of his science. His chief researches were into the phenomena of Nature, and he made minute study of rocks, plants, animal form and movement, the stars and the morphology of the Earth. He was interested in human behaviour, and wrote about character, relationships and politics. He lectured on ethics, morality, religion, psychology, grammar and the techniques of persuasion. To all this work he applied a research method of his own, partly derived from the techniques of Socrates and Plato (who discussed each topic in a way designed to strip away inessentials until a core of 'truth' was left) and partly anticipating modern scientific method. He and his assistants amassed as much information as was available about each chosen topic, studying first-hand evidence and reading all writings and opinions they could find. From this mass of material, by a rigorous process of logic, they formulated theories and principles, testing them against other people's views and new evidence as it came along. The method could be applied equally well to physical phenomena (such as variations in types of rock or animal behaviour), to abstractions (such as the nature of change or what 'virtue' is) and to human artefacts (such as political constitutions), and it was open-ended, allowing scope for alternative opinions and for constant reassessment.

Poetics

Poetics appeared some time in the 330s. In Aristotle's catalogue it was a minor work, probably unrevised and possibly incomplete. Like others of his surviving writings, it is less a polished and finished book than notes, possibly assembled for the lecture-room. It is repetitive, stylistically inconsistent and veers between passages which are fully written out and others where complex arguments are compressed into single sentences or phrases. Comparisons with other artforms, for example painting and sculpture, are tantalising as much for their brevity as their acuity. The appeal of *Poetics* is partly for the pithiness and mind-expanding nature of its pronouncements – Aristotle must have been an inspired teacher – and partly because it is the earliest piece of literary criticism from the ancient world, closer in time than any other to the artform it discusses. For modern readers, a second point of attraction is the wild way it was misinterpreted by later theorists on drama (notably in the Renaissance), and the overwhelming influence that their views – not always Aristotle's – had on subsequent dramatic theory and practice. *Poetics* may be hard, at times, to relate to the practice of Aeschylus, Sophocles and Euripides in their surviving plays, and both Aristotle's theories and those derived from them may sometimes appear eccentric or wrong, but the book is seminal for Western drama.

The Nature and Purpose of the Arts

In the last book of his *Republic*, produced some forty years before *Poetics*, Plato brought to a conclusion a

series of meditations on the nature and purpose of the
arts, meditations which had preoccupied him for half a
century. In summary, he said that if you believe that the
prime human objectives are to discover what 'virtue' is
and then aspire to it, you should deal only in truth, in
actuality. Since the arts, by definition, are confected,
they are distracting at best and at worst destructive.
God creates the ideal – for example the ideal of a table
or the ideal of 'virtue'; human beings create practical
examples of that ideal – a functional table or a life
'virtuously' lived; art creates merely a simulacrum of
such examples – a picture of a table or a 'virtuous'
dramatic character. Furthermore, the arts encourage
emotional response, far from the rational and
considered stance of the genuine seeker after truth.

In *Poetics*, briefly and bluntly, Aristotle challenges
this view. The pleasure offered by the arts – something
Plato deplored – is, for him, a moral and didactic force.
We see imitations of reality and compare them with
reality; this is both pleasurable in itself and also morally
instructive. From infancy human beings learn by
imitation, and the process does not stop with maturity,
but is ironically layered and enhanced by it. The
pleasure, and the learning, are similar whether what is
imitated is 'good' or 'bad' – discrimination in the
beholder is the deciding factor. The chief duty of
artists is to provide imitations technically as perfect as
they can make them, and in *Poetics* Aristotle offers
hints and suggestions for how this should be done,
at least in literature. The starting-point may be moral
or aesthetic philosophy, but *Poetics* is for the most part
a discussion of 'best practice' in the literary artforms.
Aristotle rates highest, of those he discusses, tragedy
and epic.

The moral implications of all this must have been even
sharper for Aristotle's audiences than they are for us
today. By his time, in his opinion at least, theatrical
writing had become jaded and degenerate, falling far
short of the aims and achievements of the previous

century. The work of Aeschylus, Sophocles, Euripides and others, so far from being a goal to which other writers aspired, had come to be regarded as out of tune with the sensibilities and style of the new generation; spectacle had begun to take the place of substance. In part, this process reflected a change – felt by many thinkers as a decline – in the moral status of the Athenian population itself. The people of today were not the equals of their parents, grandparents and especially the great-great-grandparents who had defeated the Persians and ushered in the era of Pericles, the Parthenon, Thucydides, Pheidias and Socrates. Plato's attack on the arts, in part, was for fostering and abetting this perceived decline; Aristotle in *Poetics* seems persistently to imply, without ever saying explicitly, that if more writers of the present followed the routes taken by geniuses of the past – routes he sets out in detail – both drama and its spectators would be far healthier.

The Place of Logic

Aristotle's guiding principles throughout *Poetics* are his passions for logic and for order. This is seen most obviously in his remarks on form and content. A work of art should be a unified and congruent whole, eliminating the random and of a size appropriate to its content (page 12). Length in tragedy should be measured not by arbitrary means such as clocks – though if it is, the writers should accommodate their work in a shapely manner – but by the needs of the material (page 12). There are six constituent parts of tragedy (page 10), six types of recognition scene (page 22), half a dozen kinds of choral utterance (page 16) – and they can be placed in hierarchical order according to specific logical criteria. Character-drawing is a schematic skill, articulating themes and ideas in ways which can be codified and learned (page 20). The argument about whether epic or tragedy is the nobler form of art can take place according to exact rules of rhetoric, each side balancing the other (page 40). There are a dozen ways of countering hostile criticism (page 37).

A modern writer might comment that all this is fine and fair enough, that Aristotle's summaries and recipes are persuasive, but that they still add up to a critic's and not an artist's view of how art is made. The arts in general, and performing arts in particular allow far more room than he seems to acknowledge for nuance, surprise, irony, inflection and challenge. By the nature of theatre, drama is ironical from start to finish, and the space between performers and spectators is essential to the medium, allowing an interplay of thought and response which is not apparent in the written text but which gives the performed work its life. Aristotle's claim (page 41) that tragedy makes just as much effect when read as when experienced in the theatre does not take into account that the two effects, while of similar intensity, may still be of a completely different kind. A great tragedy, a *King Lear* or an *Elektra*, say, is precisely *not* the same play in the theatre and on the page. Aristotle talks of critical distance in his discussion of 'imitation' (page 5), and has a sharp appreciation of metaphor, at least in its literary manifestations (page 30); it would have been instructive to have had his views – directly answering Plato's offensive against the arts – on the wider aesthetic question of the nature and force of metaphor in life in general, of the respective merits of 'truth' and 'fiction' as ways of articulating our whole imaginative and emotional relationship with the world around us.

Universal Order and *Hamartia*

It was axiomatic in Aristotelian thinking that chaos is inferior to order and that there is an orderly, organic progression from one state to the other. By implication, everything in the universe and in human imagination has its hierarchy. In *Poetics* men are superior to women and both are superior to slaves. 'Good' people are superior to 'bad' people, and the reasons can be defined. (Aristotle's main reason why the hero of a tragedy should be a person of distinction is that only such a person's fall from eminence is morally instructive; we are not moved by reversal in 'little' lives. It has taken over two millennia for this view to be challenged in Western literary fiction, first in novels and then, much more recently, in 'serious' drama.) Universal order depends, in part, on everyone and everything in creation maintaining its hierarchical position – if gods descend to the level of mortals, for example, or mortals aspire to the condition of gods, order is replaced by chaos. Universal order is like an embroidered cloth in which each stitch has its place; if one stitch is dropped or the cloth is torn, the whole is damaged and must be repaired.

This tearing of the cloth is what Aristotle means by *hamartia*. The word was originally used of 'falling short' in archery or spear-throwing, but came to mean any lapse from the ideal state of things, any missing of any target or error of judgment. If you tripped over a stone or called someone by the wrong name or spilt crumbs or lost your way in the street, this was *hamartia*. On a larger scale, but essentially no different, were such actions as committing a crime, blaspheming or wilfully taking any course which you knew to be wrong. Because all these forms of *hamartia* were, in essence, no more than dropped stitches in universal order, they could be put right by simple reversal of the circumstances: you picked up what you'd spilled, withdrew your blasphemy, admitted your crime, corrected your error and so restored the universal pattern.

Myth, that repository of moral and ethical instances, was full of situations where such *hamartia* had occurred, and showed the immediate results and the efforts needed to put matters right. The Trojan War, for example, could be traced back to a single 'dropped stitch' – it might be Hecuba's refusal to kill the new-born child she had been told would destroy her city and her people, or the events leading up to the Judgement of Paris, or Paris' abduction of Helen, or any of a dozen other events – but the ripple-effect from that beginning was unstoppable and led inexorably to catastrophe. The story of the royal houses of Argos or Thebes, or the myth of Herakles, evolved in similarly organic fashion from a single triggering event through an entire sequence of disaster, until the first dropped stitch was at last caught up and harmony was restored.

In all this, the correction of error is a matter less of morality than of logic. Each slip has its logical and inevitable correction, and once it is made the matter is ended. In tragedy, Kreon's condemning to death of Antigone is such a slip, and it can be corrected only by the death of another character, Haimon; Kreon's personal suffering is not enough of a corrective. It may be part of his learning process but it does not serve to restore the pattern. Oedipus' blindness to Fate is corrected by Teiresias; his physical blinding is a personal reaction, and not essential. Herakles' madness is a necessary stage in the correction of the dropped stitch which forced a god to assume human form; its effects on him and his mortal wife and children are incidental. Myth tells these tales objectively, allowing us to speculate about cause and effect but to experience only casual emotional involvement. Tragedy, by focusing on the personal anguish involved in the restoration of universal order, involves us emotionally in the characters and the situation, and so encourages us to reflect on their and our relationship with the harmony of the universe; but in the Aristotelian world-view this result, however desirable, is not part of the overriding pattern but merely an ironical, critical response to it, as when we look at the picture of 'something disgusting' (page 6), appreciate it and learn from it.

Hamartia in the Renaissance

Christian scholars who rediscovered *Poetics* in the
Renaissance completely changed Aristotle's philosophy,
throwing into it ideas which have affected dramatic
criticism, and the criticism of Greek drama in particular,
ever afterwards. In Olympian religious philosophy, the
restoration of order is enough to satisfy the gods. Logic
is observed, the disturbance is forgotten and serenity
returns. In the Judeo-Christian system, by contrast,
God must be actively involved in the process of
redemption. And in order for this to happen human
beings must first acknowledge their guilt. In the
Renaissance, therefore, *hamartia* was interpreted as
failure of a specific moral kind: Oedipus, Kreon,
Herakles were guilty, and the process of restitution
(which led in turn to the plays' moral and religious
message) involved them in realising their guilt and
atoning for it, in their suffering becoming a kind of
penance consequent upon confession. In this view,
hamartia is moral blindness, and *anagnorisis*
('recognition' or 'discovery'), which in Aristotle is a
simple matter of someone becoming aware of a fact or
a relationship previously unrealised (page 15), is trans-
formed into something entirely different: the point
where the penitent realises and admits both personal
moral guilt and the need for penance and redemption.
In fact the Renaissance overlaid the *Poetics* with a moral
structure it was never intended to have; the result is
that the *Poetics* was seen as it were through a distorting
mirror. And it is these ideas, far more morally didactic
than anything actually in *Poetics*, that have seeped into
our Western view of the nature and purpose of tragedy,
perhaps to the benefit of the art; but they have nothing
to do with Aristotle or with the plays and epic poems
which were his subject. Applying the new criteria to
ancient Athenian drama led scholars to invent a new
kind of hierarchy of playwrights altogether, in which
Aeschylus (thanks to the grand moral reflections of, in
particular, his *Oresteia*) and Sophocles (thanks to the

perceived pieties of his *Antigone* and *Oedipus Tyrannos*)
were lauded far above the nagging, morally ambiguous
and challenging Euripides. Such judgements would
have bemused both the ancient dramatists and their
audiences.

The Three Unities

The second most influential idea grafted on to *Poetics*
by Renaissance critics was the theory of the Three
Unities, Action, Place and Time. Aristotle does talk of
the Unity of Action: the events of a tragedy should have
internal coherence and inevitability, following one logical
sequence from beginning to conclusion (page 11).
To this Renaissance critics added the Unity of Place
(everything which happens should take place in a single
location – page 13) and the Unity of Time (the events
of the play should take place in a single time-span,
preferably of no more than twenty-four hours – not
quite what Aristotle says on page 12). As it happens,
these Unities are observed in the majority of the
ancient tragedies which survive to us. But the facts are
that, first, they are not followed in all of them – the
Unity of Place is ignored in Aeschylus' *Eumenides* and
Sophocles' *Aias*; the articulation of time in such plays as
Aeschylus' *Persians* or Euripides' *Women of Troy* has
nothing to do with Renaissance Unity – and, second,
that the surviving plays are no more than a fraction of
the total number written, suggest that the Unities were
not as crucial for Athenian dramaturgy as some modern
scholars, and their students, still imagine.

Kenneth McLeish, 1997

Translator's Note

The main objectives of this translation are ease
of reading and understanding. I have slightly expanded
sentences here and there, and added section headings,
plus a few editorial notes and remarks in square
brackets. The numbers in round brackets are those of
the standard chapter-divisions, not Aristotle's but a
convenience of modern scholarship. Some passages of
the original – for example Aristotle's long section on
language and grammar, pages 27-33, chiefly of interest
to speakers of ancient Greek – are printed in smaller
type (a strategy borrowed with gratitude from The Blue
Guides) as are a number of the interpolations and asides
which suggest, more than anything else, that *Poetics*
was less an edited text than a set of lecture-notes. A few
passages are printed in bold: these are the nuggets of
Aristotle's wisdom and represent summations of what
have become his most-quoted tenets. Readers should
therefore be able to navigate through the text choosing
their own level of engagement.

For Further Reading

For further reading, those interested in the philosophical aspects of Aristotle's work are referred to Malcolm Heath's Penguin Classics translation of *Poetics* (Viking, London, 1996) and to Stephen Halliwell's scholarly study, *Aristotle's Poetics* (Duckworth, London, 1986). For translations of the surviving plays from the Ancient Greek theatre, I recommend two complete series, the Methuen Classical Greek Dramatists (English accented) and the University of Pennsylvania Press Greek Drama Series (American accented). J. Michael Walton's *Living Greek Theatre: a Handbook of Classical Performance and Modern Production* (Greenwood Press, 1987) is a useful, comprehensive guide. Of the many studies of Greek tragedy by modern scholars, one of the best is still H.D.F. Kitto's *Greek Tragedy* (Methuen, London, third edition, 1961).

Poetics

Introduction

(1) My subject is literary and dramatic composition. I shall discuss the art in general and the characteristics of each of its individual forms. I shall describe how the basic elements (*muthos*) should be assembled to produce a successful composition, the number and nature of the work's constituent parts, and all other relevant matters. And I shall begin, as you might expect, with first principles.

Imitation

The chief purpose of all composition – epic, tragedy, comedy, dithyramb, the majority of instrumental music for flute or lyre – is the imitation (*mimesis*) of reality. Types of composition differ from one another, however, in three ways: the means they use, the things they imitate and the different ways they imitate the same things.

Just as some people, naturally gifted or as a result of experience, use colour and form to make imitations of reality, and others use the power of speech, so the artforms listed above use rhythm, language and melody, either individually or in combination. Flute-playing, lyre-playing and other activities of the kind (for example reed-pipe-playing) use rhythm and melody. Dancers use rhythm alone without melody, employing rhythmic movement to imitate what people are like (*ethos*), what happens to them (*pathos*) and what they do (*praxis*).

We have in Greek so far no word for the art-form which imitates reality by words alone, without melody, in prose or the various forms of verse. [The word 'literature', of Latin origin, came later.] What single word can encompass on the one hand Sophron's and Xenarchos' dramatic sketches of everyday life (*mimoi*), and on the other Socratic dialogue? We categorise poets by the kind of metres they use rather than by what they imitate: an 'epic' poet writes in epic metre, an 'elegiac' poet in elegiac metres or iambics. Even when people write medical or scientific treatises, so long as they write in verse we call them 'poets'. Homer and Empedokles have nothing in common except that they write in verse; one is a poet, the other a scientist, and so they should be called. Someone who uses a mishmash of metres to produce a literary imitation of reality – as Chairemon does in his rhapsody *Centaur* – should simply be called 'poet'.

Other art-forms, dithyramb, sacred music accompanied by the lyre, tragedy and comedy, use all three techniques listed above, rhythm, melody and language. Sometimes they are deployed together, sometimes separately and independently.

To sum up so far: the difference between one art-form and another is not in the fact of imitation, but in the means used to do it.

(2) Imitations are made of actions. The people doing or suffering these actions must be 'good' or 'bad' – the standard moral distinction between members of the human race. It follows that the people imitated must be 'better' than us, 'worse' than us, or exactly the same. The same distinction applies in fine art: Polygnotos' creations idealise reality, Pauson's caricature it and Dionysios' represent it faithfully. The distinctions are made in each of the arts, so much so that the chosen point of difference can even define an art-form. As in dancing, flute-playing and lyre-playing, so it is in literature: Homer's imitations are idealised, Kleophon's faithful, and those of Hegemon of Thasos (who invented the parody form) and Nikochares (author of the *Gallery of Lowlife*) are caricatures. The distinctions apply in dithyramb and *nomoi* [religious song], where the individuals imitated may be as different as the

Cyclops depicted by Timotheos and the Cyclops of
Philoxenos. Tragedy and comedy, too, observe them.
Tragic characters idealise reality, comic characters
caricature it.

(3) A third difference in these art-forms lies in the way
each kind of imitation [that is, of people 'worse' than
us, 'better' than us or exactly the same as us] is made. If
the things to be imitated and the means of imitation are
the same, three strategies of imitation are available: (a)
to move between narrative and assumed character, as
Homer does; (b) to remain the same throughout; (c)
to make it appear that the characters imitated are,
throughout, physically doing what is being shown.

As I said earlier, content, method and style are the three
areas of difference in artistic imitation. It follows from
this that, if we take Sophocles as an example, he
resembles Homer in one respect, that both imitate
[what I have called] 'good' people, and in another
resembles Aristophanes, in that both imitate people in
action, doing things – the reason why, according to
some, plays are called 'dramas' [literally, 'things done'].

This [use of the word 'drama'], in passing, is also the reason
why the Dorians claim that they [and not the Athenians]
invented both tragedy and comedy. Comedy was claimed
both by the town of Megara, soon after it became a democ-
racy [in the early 600s BC, when the autocrat Theagenes was
exiled], and by the Megarian-founded town of Megara
Hyblaia in Sicily, on the grounds that Epicharmos [late sixth
century BC] came from there and lived [two generations]
before Chionides and Magnes [early fifth-century Athenian
writers of comedy]. Other Dorian towns in the Peloponnese
[notably Sikyon] claim tragedy. In all cases, their supporting
evidence is linguistic, the words 'comedy' and 'drama'
themselves. They call their outlying villages *komai*, not
'demes' as in Athens, and this, not the word *komazein* ['to
revel'] is the origin of comedy, the performers moving from
village to village when they were not appreciated in town
itself. Similarly, their word for 'to do' is *dran* [hence *drama*,
something done], whereas in Athens people say *prattein*
[whose derivative for 'something done' is *pragma*].

So much for the various different kinds of imitation.

Origins and Early Development of Drama

(4) There are probably two sources of dramatic composition, both rooted in human nature and behaviour. The instinct for imitation is characteristic of human beings from earliest childhood. We imitate far more than any other species, our earliest learning is by imitation, and we enjoy imitations of all kinds, even of things which are disgusting, even of dead bodies. The reason is that discovery, learning things, gives pleasure not only to the intellectually-minded but to all of us, of whatever mental ability. When we look at pictures, our pleasure may be in recognising the subjects – 'That's so-and-so' – or, even if we've no idea who the subject is, it may be in such matters as the artist's style, the colours used, or things like that.

Our natural instinct for imitation, coupled with those for melody and rhythm (of which metre is an organised development), led to improvisations which gradually evolved and became more sophisticated until people began composing verse literature. This very quickly diverged into two main kinds, depending on the inclination of the creator. Serious-minded creators imitated 'elevated' actions and the 'elevated' characters who performed them. Less serious-minded creators imitated the actions of less 'elevated' characters, turning to satire as naturally as their serious colleagues did to choral hymns [invocations of the gods, or descriptions of their deeds and attributes] and praise-poems [similar pieces about high-achieving real people, in war, politics or athletics contests: Pindar's *Odes* are typical]. Satire probably existed long before Homer, but none survives; the first we know of are Homer's own *Margites* [a poem now lost, satirising a self-made intellectual who knew snippets about a vast range of matters, but understood none of it] and a clutch of poems by others from the same period. These works used the iambic metre [da-DAH, da-DAH, da-DAH, and so on] – hence the current meaning of the word *iambizein*, 'to set about someone'.

So, some authors of the past were serious, others comic.
Homer however is unique: he was not only outstanding
at serious work, thanks to his literary and dramatic
excellence, but also laid the foundations for comedy by
replacing mere invective with a dramatic imitation of
the ridiculous. His *Margites* stands in the same relation
to later comedy as do his *Iliad* and *Odyssey* to later
tragedy.

As soon as tragedy and comedy evolved – grander and
more valued forms of art than the epic and satire which
had preceded them, authors were drawn to them, each
by their respective inclination. Those who favoured
satire composed comedy, those who favoured epic
turned to tragedy.

I don't propose to discuss here the question of whether
tragedy has reached its 'perfect' state, in relation both to
theory and stage practice. That is a matter for separate
investigation.

Both tragedy and comedy originated in improvisation,
tragedy with the prelude to the dithyramb [thought to
be improvised by the leader of the Chorus before the
author's actual text began], and comedy with the
prelude to the 'phallic songs' [ribald, satirical choruses]
which are still traditional in many areas. Tragedy then
developed gradually, as authors experimented with and
improved each new idea that came along. Development
stopped when it reached its natural form. Aeschylus was
first to increase the number of actors from one to two,
in the process cutting back the amount of chorus-work
and giving pre-eminence to spoken dialogue. Sophocles
was first to use three actors and painted scenery.
[A typical example of such development is the way]
tragedy gradually acquired its size [by which I mean
both length and artistic density]. When it moved out of
its satyr-phase, it abandoned their anecdotal plots and
undignified language, and its principal metre became
iambic rather than trochaic [DAH-da, DAH-da, DAH-
da, and so on]. Trochaic metre was ideal for the style

and dance of satyrs, but as soon as dialogue appeared, Nature herself supplied the appropriate metre. Iambics are close to ordinary speech, as is obvious when you think how often we fall into them in ordinary conversation – unlike hexameters [the metre of epic poetry like Homer's], which we rarely use in conversation unless we are trying to make a specific effect.

A fourth development was the increase in the number of units in each play [that is, dialogue scenes, lyric scenes and choruses]. There were other improvements [changes in masks, costumes, choreography and so on], but it would take too long to go through all the stages in detail, so I take them as understood.

(5) **Comedy.** When I said that comedy is the imitation of people 'worse' than the average, this implied not total moral degeneracy but a falling from the ideal into one single form of such degeneracy, the ridiculous. The ridiculous can be defined as a mistake or a lapse from 'perfection' which causes no pain or serious harm to others. An obvious example is the comic mask, which is distorted and 'imperfect' but not so as to cause pain.

For tragedy, the stages of development and their causes are well known. Comedy is more mysterious, because at the start no one took it seriously. It was only at a late stage in its development [possibly in 465BC] that it was granted official state commissions [literally, 'choruses'] at the dramatic festivals; until then, performances were casual. By the time of this development, several of its traditions were well-established.

No one knows who first introduced masks, prologues, more than one actor and other such changes. We do know that the idea of an invented plot originated in Sicily with Epicharmos and Phormis, and that in Athens [in the mid-fifth century] Krates was the first author to replace loose lampoon with structured plot and dialogue.

Epic poetry and tragedy. These are alike only in this respect, that they use dignified verse to show imitations of serious subjects. They differ in two main ways. **Epic is in narrative style and uses the same verse metre throughout, and its action has no fixed time-span, while that of tragedy is normally a single twenty-four-hour period, or just over.** This was a late development; originally tragedy and epic were the same in their use of time. The components of the two forms also differ. Some they share, others are unique to tragedy. Anyone who can judge between good tragedy and bad can do the same for epic, because every component in epic is also present in tragedy. All the components of tragedy, however, are not to be found in epic.

The Constituent Elements of Tragedy

(6) I'll deal later with imitation in epic and with comedy. In what follows, I want to discuss tragedy. First, to summarise what has been said so far about its nature: **tragedy is the imitation of an action which is serious, complete and substantial. It uses language enriched in different ways, each appropriate to its part [of the action]. It is drama [that is, it shows people performing actions] and not narration. By evoking pity and terror it brings about the purgation (*catharsis*) of those emotions.**

By language which is 'enriched' I mean metrically organised speech and song, and by 'each appropriate to its part' I mean that some parts are spoken and others sung.

Actors perform the imitation. Spectacle is the first essential part of this performance. Other parts include their language and their lyrical ability. By 'language' I mean the way they perform the spoken passages; 'lyrical ability' is self-explanatory. And further: actors in their performance imitate specific qualities of character and reason, those crucial factors in the success or failure of all human action. In a play, what is action in real life becomes *muthos*, that is, an ordered sequence of events; character becomes an imitation of what the people of the story are like; reason is shown when they tell us or show us what is in their minds.

To sum up. Tragedy depends for its effect on six constituent elements: plot, character, language, thought, the visual, and music. These are the ingredients of tragedy, used by practically all dramatists; there are no others.

Of all these elements, plot or *muthos* is the most important. [Unlike a picture], a tragedy is not an imitation of people's appearance, but of their actions, joys, sorrows – their lives. These are what dramatists set out to show, not moral qualities. Just as, in life, moral qualities make us who we are but what we do determines the nature of our existence, so in plays the characters' actions are all-important, and their moral qualities are reflected in those actions. *Muthos* [the way the material is organised] comes first in tragedy and is all-important. Without it, there *is* no tragedy – something which cannot be said of character-analysis. In fact, many recent playwrights dispense with it altogether. Their work is a dramatic equivalent of the style of the portrait-maker Zeuxis, who depicts people without individual character, as compared with the characterful style of Polygnotos. You can write a sequence of speeches full of character, reason and elegant expression, and still create a less effective tragedy than someone who fails in all those qualities but still has a convincing *muthos*. Two of the essential ingredients of tragedy, *peripeteia* ['reversal', see page 15] and *anagnorisis* ['discovery' or 'recognition', see page 15] are functions of *muthos*. Beginners are often better at dialogue and character than organisation of the *muthos* – something which applies to most of the earliest tragic dramatists. *Muthos* is the soul of drama, just as in painting an outline sketch will predominate over a haphazard conglomeration of even the loveliest colours.

Plays imitate actions first, character second and reason
third. By 'reason' I mean the ability to express the range
of options in each situation and to choose the most
appropriate. In tragedy, this comes in the spoken
dialogue; in life it is what politicians and trained
rhetoricians do. In earlier tragedies characters spoke like
politicians [that is, using common-sense insight and
natural flair in persuasion]; in modern tragedies they
talk like rhetoricians [that is, people trained to organise
and present arguments specifically for one side or the
other of an issue]. Just as character reveals the moral
status of people making deliberate choices about courses
of action where none are obvious (for if no choice is to
be made, no character is required), so reason is revealed
in a speech where someone argues for one side or
another, or utters an informed opinion of any kind.

The fourth element, language, is the arrangement of
words to express meaning, and is the same in
imaginative literature [literally 'verse', with which I am
exclusively dealing here] and practical writing [literally
'prose', the medium for factual description and
analysis]. Of the other elements, lyricism is the chief
enrichment of tragedy. The visual, the way the dramatic
event looks, is important but not essential to artistic
meaning. Tragedy can make its effect independently of
performance, and the look of a stage production has
more to do with the stage-manager than with the
author.

Muthos (1)

(7) Having defined the parts, let me move on to discuss
muthos, the organisation of events, since this is the chief
component of tragedy. We are agreed that **tragedy is
the imitation of an action which is a whole,
completed and substantial. (Something can be
complete without being substantial.) By 'whole'
I mean that it has a beginning, a middle and an
end.** A beginning is something which does not follow

or result from anything else but after which something else follows or results. An end is the mirror-image of this: something which follows or results from something else, but which nothing else results from or follows. A middle follows something else and itself is followed. A properly-organised *muthos* should not begin at random or end at random; it should observe the rules just stated.

If something is to be considered beautiful, whether it is natural or created, its component parts must not only be well arranged but must have individual substance: beauty itself consists of substance and arrangement. A tiny creature, which we would see so briefly that our senses would have no time to take it fully in, would not have beauty, any more than an enormous creature – say, 1000km long – which we could never see at a single moment and could therefore never take in as a single entity. And just as living things should have substance but still be comprehensible, so too with the *muthos* of a tragedy: it must be substantial but easily comprehended.

The restrictions on length imposed by the circumstances of festivals and public competitions are irrelevant to my argument. If the rules decreed that a hundred tragedies were to be performed in a given time, their length would be determined by the clock – apparently this once happened. But the actual nature of the action [imitated] imposes boundaries of its own. Providing a story is comprehensible, it can be as long as its substance and quality demand. As a rule of thumb, a length which allows the hero to move, in an inevitable or plausible sequence of events, from bad fortune to good or from good to bad, is the right length for the substance of the story.

(8) Some people maintain, wrongly, that a *muthos* has unity if it centres on a single individual. Many things, indeed countless things, happen to an individual, some of which are not part of a single, unified [sequence of events]; an individual does many things which cannot

be made into a single [unified sequence of action]. In my view, all those authors who have produced *The Adventures of Herakles*, *The Adventures of Theseus* or similar works are misguided. They assume that their work has unity because it centres on a single individual (eg Herakles). Homer had it right, by art or by natural genius standing far above all others in this as in every other respect. His *Odyssey* does not describe everything that ever happened to Odysseus, but has unity of the kind I have described, omitting events which have no essential or likely relevance (for example the occasion when Odysseus was wounded on Mount Parnassos and his pretence of madness when the lords come to recruit him for the expedition against Troy). The same is true of the *Iliad*. Just as in other representational arts, 'unity of imitation' means that a single subject is imitated, so in literature **the *muthos* must imitate a single, unified and complete sequence of action.** Its incidents must be organised in such a way that if any is removed or has its position changed, the whole is dislocated and disjointed. If something can be added or taken away without any obvious effect, it is not intrinsic to the whole.

(9) It is clear from all this that the job of an author of fiction is to write not about what actually happens but about what might or should happen in a given set of circumstances. The distinction between a writer of history and an author of drama or epic is not that the historian writes in prose and the others in verse. You could rework Herodotos' *Researches into the Causes and Events of the Persian Wars* in verse and it would make no difference to its status as history. The real difference is that the historian describes reality (past events) and the others possibility. You could say that it follows from this that drama and epic are more scientific and intellectually rigorous than history, since their subjects are 'universals' [general truths] rather than 'particulars' [specific incidents]. By 'universals' I mean what people might do or say, necessarily or probably, because of who

and what they are. Drama and epic do this even when
they give the characters 'real' names. By 'particulars'
I mean what actual people – Alkibiades, for example –
did or said in reality.

[Although both comedy and tragedy deal in 'universals', there
is a practical difference between them.] In comedy, writers
invent their plots, sequences of probable events, and then
make up names for their characters. (This is quite different
from earlier satirists, who lampooned specific named individuals.) Tragedy [by contrast,] does use 'real' names [that is,
those of characters from pre-existing myth]. The reason is
that we believe in the possible, and past events [such as those
recounted in myth] have [in a sense] already happened and
are therefore more plausible than events which are still in the
future. If they had not been possible, they would not have
happened. [The use of 'real' names thus helps us to believe in
what is happening onstage.] However, in some tragedies only
one or two names are 'real' and the others are invented; other
works, such as Agathon's popular *Antheus*, use entirely
invented plots and names. There is no need for tragedians
always to use traditional stories, and it would be absurd to
expect it. The stories we think of as 'familiar' are familiar to
only a few people, but appeal to everyone.

It follows from all this that, since dramatists are creating
imitations, and what they are imitating is action, they
should think of themselves as devisers of *muthos* as
much as of lines of verse. Even if they imitate what has
actually happened, they are still creating it, in the sense
that nothing prevents what has actually happened from
also being bound to happen or likely to happen – and
that is the aspect which interests the writer as creator.

The kind of episodic *muthos* where there is no probable or
likely sequence of action is the least satisfactory of all. Bad
authors invent them because they can do no better. Good
authors write them because of practical constraints [literally
'because of the actors'], stretching the *muthos* beyond its
capacity to suit [the requirements of] a particular
performance and being forced to distort its [logical]
continuity. Tragedy represents not merely a complete action
but also incidents meant to arouse pity and terror, and these
incidents have more effect if, however unexpected they seem,
they follow the logic of the whole sequence than if they

occur by chance or simply for their own sakes. Even accidents seem more amazing if there appears to be an element of [logical] purpose in them: as for example when the man responsible for Mitys' death was watching a show in Argos, and the statue of Mitys there fell on his head and killed him. We like to think that such events are 'more than accidents' – and this kind of logic, similarly, improves a *muthos*.

(10) Just as a sequence of action can be simple or complex, so can the *muthos* which imitates it. A 'simple' action is single and continuous as described above, but the change of fortune in it happens without reversal or discovery. In a 'complex' action, the change involves discovery and reversal, and these should arise from the organisation of the *muthos*: that is, there should be an inevitable or plausible link between what happens and what follows. The difference is important between something happening *because* of something else, and something happening merely *after* it.

Reversal and Discovery (1)

(11) Reversal (*peripeteia*), as I said above, is when the circumstances change to their direct opposite – and it, too, should be inevitable or plausible. An example is in [Sophocles'] *Oedipus Tyrannos* when the Corinthian comes to bring Oedipus the good news that he no longer need fear [marrying] his mother – and when, by revealing the truth of Oedipus' parentage, he does exactly the opposite of what he intends. In *Lynkeus* [by the fourth-century tragedian Theodektes, a play now lost], a man is led off to execution, Danaos follows to kill him, and then, as a result of earlier events, Danaos is killed and Lynkeus survives.

Discovery (*anagnorisis*), as the word suggests, is a change from ignorance to knowledge. Those destined to change their fortunes from good to bad or bad to good discover that they have had a close relationship or been enemies in the past. Such discoveries are best when linked with reversal, as happens in *Oedipus Tyrannos*. Of course, other kinds of discovery are possible – for example when references are made to unimportant matters or to the fact that someone has done or not done something. But the kind of discovery which is integral to the *muthos* and involves reversal of fortune, as described above, not only involves pity or terror, those essential elements (as I see it) of tragic imitation, but is also the hinge on which good fortune turns to bad and vice versa.

If there is discovery there must be a discoverer. Sometimes only one character is involved in the discovery, and the other's identity is known. In other cases each of the parties is involved in discovering the other. In [Euripides'] *Iphigeneia in Tauris*, Orestes' discovery of Iphigeneia's identity is made when her letter is delivered to him, but a completely separate discovery is required to reveal his identity to her.

Reversal and discovery are the first two plot-elements which hinge on such incidents. They are as discussed. The third element is suffering (*pathos*): that is, a painful or fatal incident, such as death onstage, maiming or extreme torment. [On this, see chapters 13 and 14 below.]

The Components of Tragedy

(12) In chapter 6 I described the six constituent elements of tragedy. In terms of dramatic structure, plays are divided up into the introduction, episode, conclusion and choral songs. These occur in all tragedies; in some there are also songs by the actors and *kommoi* (see below). The prologue is everything in a tragedy which comes before the *parodos*. Episodes are the parts which appear between choral songs. The finale (*exodos*) is the part of the tragedy not followed by a choral song. In the choral parts, *parodos* is the entrance-song, *stasima* are odes. *Kommos* is a scene of musical lamentation shared between actor[s] and Chorus. These are the structural components of tragedy, to be used together with the constituent elements mentioned in chapter 6.

Muthos (2)

(13) Our next questions are these. When constructing a
muthos, what should writers aim for? What should they
avoid? How can the object of tragedy be best achieved?

We are assuming that t**he best kinds of *muthos* for
tragedy are not simple but complex, and are
devised to represent incidents which arouse pity
and terror.** It follows from this that three kinds of
muthos should be avoided. (a) We should not show a
good man moving from happiness to unhappiness.
Instead of arousing pity or terror, this repels. (b) We
should not show a bad man moving from unhappiness
to happiness. This is the least dramatic choice available,
fulfilling none of the requirements of tragedy and
neither appealing to our human instinct [for natural
justice] nor arousing pity or terror in us. (c) We should
not show a scoundrel moving from happiness to
unhappiness. This may appeal to our instinct [for
justice] but will arouse neither pity (since that happens
when the hero's suffering is undeserved) nor terror
(since that happens when the hero is someone like
ourselves).

The heroes who remain lie between all these. They are
not saints, but their sufferings are caused less by innate
wickedness than because of *hamartia* ('error'). [See
Introduction, page xi. *Hamartia* is the failing in
understanding or moral character which leads someone
to a disastrous choice of action: a choice which arouses
our pity because it is both catastrophic and made
deliberately but not out of wickedness, and arouses our
terror because we identify with both the innocence and
the helplessness of the person who makes the choice.]
**Heroes should be people of high degree and
reputation**: Oedipus, Thyestes, people of that kind of
distinction and from that level of society.

The outcome of a *muthos* should be single and not
double. Its movement should be not from unhappiness
to happiness but from happiness to unhappiness. The

movement should arise not from wickedness but from *hamartia* in a person of the type described or better (never worse). This last statement is confirmed by practice. Early dramatists used a wide variety of plots, but our best writers now concentrate on a handful of myths: those involving the families of Alkmaion, Oedipus, Orestes, Meleagros, Thyestes, Telephos and others who caused, or suffered, terrible events.

Since, in theory, this kind of plot is best, it is wrong for critics to complain that Euripides' plays end in unhappiness. That is what tragedy means – a fact regularly confirmed in practice, where plays of this kind (if effectively performed) are the most tragic of all. Euripides can be criticised on many other counts [see, for example, chapters 14-16, 18, 25], but there is no doubt that his plays are *tragedies*.

Unlike some authorities, who prefer it, I put second best the kind of *muthos* used in the *Odyssey*, the double *muthos* in which morally good characters end differently from morally bad ones. I think that this appeals to an audience's sentimentality, and that those writers who use it are pandering to their spectators. The pleasure it gives is that of comedy, not tragedy. In comedy, even such implacable enemies as Orestes and Aigisthos end up the best of friends, and nobody gets killed.

(14) Pity and terror can be aroused by what happens onstage. But the better authors are, the more they arrange the *muthos* to produce these reactions – and this is to be preferred. The *muthos* should be organised in such a way that even if you never see the play, but only hear an account of what happens in it, you will feel a shudder of terror and pity: this happens, for example, with the story of Oedipus. Producing the effect by performance means is less artistic and involves outside help. And to produce, by staging alone, effects which arouse no terror but are merely spectacular is to have nothing to do with tragedy. We should expect tragedy to give us not indiscriminate satisfaction but what is unique to itself.

Since the author's task is to arouse, by imitation, the satisfaction of feeling pity and terror, the ability to do this must be inherent in the incidents of the play. We need to examine what kind of incidents will result in such reactions. What is done in a play inevitably happens between people who like each other, hate each other or are indifferent to each other. If the action happens between two people who hate each other, there is nothing to pity in either what happens or the intention behind it (except possibly the suffering involved). If the people are strangers to one another, the same applies. Authors should work for situations where terrible things happen between intimates: for example, where sibling murders sibling, child parent or parent child. (The deed need not be actual killing: planning murder, or making similar plans, is sufficient.)

The traditional myth-stories should not be altered. Klytemnestra should always be killed by Orestes; Alkmaion should always kill Eriphyle. But talented authors will always find personal approaches to the stories. The phrase 'personal approaches' needs elaboration. In former times writers made their characters do what they did in full knowledge of all the facts, as Euripides does with Medea when she kills her children, or do what they did without realising the implications until later, as Sophocles did with Oedipus. (Admittedly, what Oedipus did [murdering his father, and marrying his mother] happened outside the action of the play, but similar deeds are done during the action by such characters as Astydamas' Alkmaion or Telegonos in [Sophocles'] *Odysseus Wounded*.) A third alternative is to plan the deed in full knowledge, and then not do it. A fourth is to plan some irreparable deed in ignorance and then discover the truth before you do it. There are no other possibilities. The deed must either be done or not be done; the doer must either know the truth or not know the truth.

The worst choice is [to make your character] plan the deed with full knowledge, and then not do it. This does happen occasionally – for example between Haimon and Kreon in *Antigone* [when Haimon draws his sword

to kill Kreon but Kreon escapes] – but it is inelegant
and undramatic (since there is no tragic suffering).
Slightly better is the situation where someone does the
deed without knowing the full circumstances until
afterwards [as when Agave in *Bacchae* kills Pentheus]:
there is nothing meretricious in this, and the discovery
is effective. Best of all, however, is the third alternative:
as for example in *Kresphontes* [by Euripides; now lost]
when Merope recognises her son at the very moment
she is about to kill him, or the similar situation in
[Euripides'] *Iphigeneia in Tauris* [where Iphigeneia
discovers the true identity of her brother Orestes as she
is about to kill him], or when the son in *Helle* [a play
about which nothing is now known] recognises his
mother just as he is about to hand her to her enemy.

This explains why, as I said above, tragic plots involve
such a small number of families. Authors found out by
experiment, not precept, how to produce the required
effect in their plotting, but they still must keep to the
myths in which suitable events occur.

So much for the nature and organisation of the *muthos*.

Character

(15) As regards the characters, there are four points to
aim at. First and most important, they must be 'good'.
As I said above [chapter 6], character will be displayed if
the dialogue or actions of the play show choice, and if
the choice is 'good' the character will be 'good'.
'Goodness' is possible whatever the status of the person.
Although females are inferior and slaves are beneath
consideration, both a female and a slave can be 'good'.

Second, character should be appropriate. For example,
there is a 'manly' character, and it would be
inappropriate if a female showed it, or if she showed
intellectual ability.

Third, characters should fit their 'reality'. This 'fitness' differs from both the 'goodness' and 'appropriateness' described above.

Fourth, character should be consistent. Even if the character is inconsistent in the author's source, that character in the play should be *consistently* inconsistent.

In [Euripides'] *Orestes*, Menelaos is uncharacteristically 'bad'. In *Skylla*, Odysseus is shown in tears. In [Euripides'] *Melanippe*, the heroine is shown as an intellectual. The character of Iphigeneia in [Euripides'] *Iphigeneia at Aulis* is inconsistent: [pleading for mercy] before the sacrifice and [full of courage] later in the play.

When writing characters, just as when organising the *muthos*, it is important to make everything inevitable or at least plausible. Whenever a given character says or does something, it should follow inevitably or plausibly from what we know of the character and from what has gone before.

In the same way the outcome of a *muthos* should follow logically from the action so far, and should not depend on a stage-trick, as in *Medea* [by Euripides, when a chariot, swung on the theatre-crane, arrives to take Medea out of reach of Jason's vengeance], or on events like the scene of launching the fleet in the *Iliad* [where, when Agamemnon tests his men by proposing that they launch the fleet and sail home before sacking Troy, they unexpectedly agree with him, and the goddess Athene has to swoop down from Olympos to stop them leaving]. Interventions like this should be used only to reveal matters outside the plot, for example things in the past or future which none of the mortals know, and which need therefore to be announced [by a god], since by definition the gods know everything. There should be nothing irrational about such things, or if there is it should be kept well outside the play, as Sophocles does in *Oedipus Tyrannos* [where the *muthos* is contrived so that we don't ask why Oedipus, investigating the death of Laios, never connects it with the murder he himself committed at the crossroads].

Since tragedy is an imitation of people 'better' than average, authors should do as good portrait-artists do, catching the essence of their sitters but still improving their appearance. Even if we make characters irritable or lazy, or give them other such qualities, we should always preserve their dignity – as Homer and Agathon do in their portrayals of Achilles.

These rules should be carefully observed, as indeed should the comments in my other writings about the author's responsibility for the physical appearance of what is shown on stage.

Discovery (2)

(16) I return to discovery (*anagnorisis*). I described its nature earlier [chapter 11]. There are six types of discovery:

(a) *Discovery by marks or physical objects*. This is the least artistic, and is often used because an incompetent author can think of nothing better. Some marks are inherited: the spearhead-shaped birthmark carried by all the descendants of the Sown Men of Thebes, the star-mark on the shoulders of all descendants of Pelops, used in Karkinos' [now lost] *Thyestes*. Others are acquired [after birth]: scars from wounds, say, or objects such as necklaces, or – as in Sophocles' *Tyro* [now lost: a play in which the identity of Poseidon's sons by the mortal Tyro was discovered because of the little craft in which they were floated out to sea as infants], even a boat. Discovery of this kind can be handled well or badly. An example of both occurs in the *Odyssey*, when Odysseus' hunting-scar is recognised by the servant [Eurykleia, who does so in a way arising inevitably from the plot, when she washes the stranger-visitor and finds that he is her master] and by the swineherds [Eumaios and Philoitios, in the scene where Odysseus baldly tells them who he is and then shows the scar to prove it]. Discoveries deliberately contrived are inartistic, as are all such contrivances; those involving reversal, like the bath-scene, are preferable.

(b) *Discoveries contrived by the author.* They are inartistic. In [Euripides'] *Iphigeneia in Tauris*, for example, Orestes

tells Iphigeneia who he is. Her identity is revealed to
him in the incident of the letter [when she gives
Pylades a letter to deliver to her long-lost brother
Orestes, thinking him far away in Argos, and Pylades
simply hands it to Orestes before her eyes], but Orestes
simply tells her who he is, which is what Euripides
wants but is not inherent in the *muthos*. If he had turned
up with signs and tokens, it would have been just like
type of discovery (a). Another example is when the
embroidery 'speaks' in Sophocles' *Tereus* [now lost; the
embroidery 'speaks' when Philomela, who has had her
tongue cut out to stop her telling who raped her, puts
the story in a piece of embroidery and shows it to her
sister Prokne].

(c) *Discovery by memory.* This is when something a
character sees triggers understanding. Examples are the
scene in Dikaiogenes' *The Cyprians* when Teukros is
recognised when he sees his dead father's picture and
bursts into tears, or the scene in the *Odyssey* when
Odysseus is recognised in Alkinoös' court because he
weeps to hear the minstrel [telling of the deaths of the
Greeks at Troy].

(d) *Discovery from deduction.* An example is the scene
in [Aeschylus'] *Libation-bearers* when [Elektra infers]
'Someone like me has been here [to pray at
Agamemnon's tomb]; no one is like me but Orestes;
therefore it is Orestes who has come'.

In Polyeidos' *Iphigeneia in Tauris* [now lost] what happens is
entirely plausible: that Orestes, being led out to be sacrificed,
should say that the same thing happened to his sister
[Iphigeneia, who was in fact rescued and is about to supervise
his death]. Similar scenes occur in Theodektes' *Tydeus* [now
lost] when he says 'I came to find my son, and am now to die
myself', and in *Phineus' Children* [now lost] when the women
are taken to the place where they are were exposed at birth,
and deduce that it is there they are condemned also to die.

(e) *Discovery through false deduction by the audience.* In
Odysseus Disguised [author unknown; play lost],
Odysseus says that he recognises a bow [which we have

no reason to believe that] he has ever seen, and we accept it even though it is a false deduction on our part. [Odysseus comes to Ithaka disguised, and tells everyone that 'Odysseus' died at Troy. We expect his identity to be revealed when he is the only person able to string the warbow, but in fact he reveals it by recognising the bow in the first place, something no stranger to Ithaka could ever do.]

(f) *Discovery from the events themselves.* This is the kind we find in Sophocles' *Oedipus Tyrannos* [in the scene with the Corinthian mentioned in chapter 11] and the discovery-scene in [Euripides'] *Iphigeneia in Tauris*, where it is entirely plausible that Iphigeneia would want to send a letter. This is the only kind which dispenses with such artificial aids [to discovery] as birthmarks, necklaces [or the like]. Because it arises from what is plausible, this is the best kind of discovery, though discovery from deduction comes second.

Some Practical Hints

(17) When working on *muthos* and dialogue, authors should bear three things in mind.

(a) They should visualise the action throughout. **Only by imagining events as clearly as if they were present in person can they follow the logic of what is happening** and avoid incongruity.

An example comes in Karkinos' play, where Amphiaraos is shown rising from the ground of his temple. Karkinos failed to visualise the scene and missed this fault, but in performance the audience noticed and the play failed. This fault is not obvious in the text.

(b) So far as possible, they should act out what they are writing, even down to the characters' movements and gestures. If two writers are of equal natural ability, the more convincing will be the one who [also] shares the actual emotions, blustering like a blusterer, ranting like someone furious. Writers need to have sympathetic

natures or be slightly mad. The first kind easily
understand the emotions [of the characters], the second
kind feel those emotions in person.

(c) Plays, whether on pre-existing or original stories,
should be first sketched in general outline, then fleshed
out in detail. I take the story of Iphigeneia as an
example. In outline this is as follows. 'A girl has been
offered for sacrifice, magically transported to a foreign
country and made priestess in a place where the custom
is to sacrifice strangers to the goddess. Some time later
it happens that her brother arrives there. (The fact that
a god told him to go there, and the reasons for his
journey, are irrelevant at this stage.) He arrives and is
arrested. On the point of being sacrificed he reveals his
identity, either in the way shown by Euripides or, as in
Polyeidos' play, by saying, naturally enough in the
circumstances, "So I'm to be sacrificed, just like my
sister"). They both escape.' Only when this outline is
complete should you add names and detailed scenes –
and the added material should always fit the story, for
example in this case, the attack of madness which led to
Orestes' capture and the way the escape is organised by
the purification-ritual [when Iphigeneia pretends that
Orestes has polluted the goddess' statue because he is
a murderer, and that she must take them both for
purification to the seashore – where a ship is waiting
to rescue them]. Plays require less of this fleshing-out
than epics. The plot of the *Odyssey*, for example, is
short: 'A man is away from home for years, alone and
harassed by Poseidon. Meanwhile suitors, courting his
wife, squander his property and plot to murder his son.
After many adventures he arrives home, reveals his
identity and attacks the suitors. His enemies are killed
and he survives.' That is the [basic] story; everything
else is fleshing-out.

(18) All tragedies consist of complication [*desis*, literally
'binding' or 'knotting'] and resolution [*lusis*, literally
'unfastening' or 'unknotting']. Events before the play's
first scene, and some of those in the action itself, make

the complication, and the rest of the play makes the resolution. Complication is everything from the start of the story to the moment of reversal, from misery to happiness or happiness to misery. Resolution is everything which follows that change of fortune [reversal]. In Theodektes' *Lynkeus* complication is everything up to the point where first the child is kidnapped and then his parents are arrested; the resolution is from the murder charge to the end.

Complication and resolution are two of the chief ways which make one tragedy like, or unlike, another. If they have the same complication and the same resolution, they are like. Many writers are good at complication but bad at resolution. Good writers are good at both.

[The text of the following passage is corrupt, and the translation below, which slightly reorders it, is conjecture only.] I recommend using in your play all the elements that make a good tragedy, or as many as possible. There have been writers outstanding at each of the elements, and if you concentrate on just one element critics will condemn you unfairly for falling short of the finest in the field. I distinguish four elements of interest and four kinds of tragedy which exemplify them. (a) *Complex tragedy* depends on reversal and discovery. (b) *Tragedy of suffering* is seen in plays about such people as Aias or Ixion. (c) *Character tragedy* is seen in such plays as Sophocles' *Women of Phthia* and his and Euripides' versions of the *Peleus* story [all now lost]. (d) *Tragedy of spectacle* is what we find in, say, Sophocles' *Children of Phorkys*, his *Prometheus* and any play set in the Underworld.

A tragedy, as I have often said, should not be written like an epic: that is, crammed with stories, as if one tried to put the whole *Iliad* in a single play. The *Iliad* is long enough to give each episode due attention; a single play [covering the same events] would fall far short. When writers have tried to cover the entire Trojan War in one play (rather than choosing separate incidents for separate plays, as Euripides does), or to deal with the whole Niobe myth-cycle and not merely part of it, as Aeschylus does – those writers, even including Agathon have had little or no success in performance.

In scenes of reversal, and in 'simple' plots , writers get results by using surprise: this device is both dramatic and true to human nature. I mean when a confidence-trickster like Sisyphos is outwitted or a brave scoundrel is defeated. Such surprises do not violate the rules of logic: as Agathon says, 'Even the unexpected is to be expected'.

The Chorus should be treated as one of the actors and incorporated in the plot. Writers should follow Sophocles in this, rather than Euripides. As for later authors, their choral songs will fit the plot of any tragedy. They are interludes – something else pioneered by Agathon. Interludes! You might as well take a speech or a whole scene from one play and stick it in another.

Reason and Language

(19) I now move on to other matters, reason and language.

I deal with reason more fully in my *Art of Rhetoric*. The word 'reason' includes all the effects which can be produced by language: proof or refutation of an argument, the arousal of emotions like pity, terror, anger and the others, the capacity to exaggerate and understate. Obviously, the same rules will also apply to selecting the actions to arouse pity and terror or make things seem important or plausible. The only difference is that effects in action are often explicit without needing words, whereas effects in dialogue must always be achieved verbally, since if they happened anyway who would need the dialogue?

Students of language [that is, of the way words are put together, their grammar, syntax and so on] investigate, among other things, change of meaning in a phrase or sentence through what is known as declamation, differentiating for example between orders and requests, statements and assertions, questions and answers. These are technical matters of performance expertise, and the author's knowledge or ignorance of them is hardly relevant in criticism of the work. Protagoras once objected to Homer's phrase 'Sing, goddess, of Achilles' rage' [the opening invocation of the *Iliad*] on the grounds that it was an order and not the prayer it ought to be. He was quite right – telling someone to do or not do something is certainly an order – but the whole thing has nothing to do with drama, and I say no more about it here.

(20) The phenomenon of language comprises phonemes, syllables, connectives, nouns, verbs, conjunctions, inflections and utterance.

A *phoneme* is a single, indivisible sound – but not every such sound is a phoneme, only those which can join with other sounds to make meaning-groups. Animals utter indivisible sounds, but these are not (in my opinion) phonemes. The phonemes I mean may be either vowels, continuants or mutes. A vowel is an audible sound made without connection [between the speech-organs, that is lips and tongue]. A continuant involves such connection and makes an audible sound (examples are the sounds 's' and 'r'). A mute has by itself no sound, but is audible when joined to a vowel (examples are the Greek letters gamma and delta). Phonemes differ according to the shape made by the mouth, the point of connection, whether they have aspiration or not, how long they are and whether they are pitched acute [rising inflexion], grave [descending inflexion] or intermediate. Detailed discussion of these differences is part of the study of poetic metre.

A *syllable* is a sound without intrinsic meaning, a combination of phoneme and mute. (For example, both 'gr' without an 'a' and 'gra' are syllables.) Once again, detailed discussion is part of the study of poetic metre.

A *connective* is either a sound without intrinsic meaning – [in Greek,] *men*, *de*, *deh*, *toee* – which neither prevents nor causes the formation of a single, meaningful sound from several sounds, and which cannot appear on its own at the beginning of a phrase, or it is a sound without intrinsic meaning which causes the formation of single, meaningful sounds from several sounds each of which has its own intrinsic meaning. [In Greek,] examples are *amfi* ['around'] and *peri* ['about'].

A *conjunction* is a sound without intrinsic meaning which marks the beginning or end of a phrase or articulates it in the middle... [text corrupt] ... It therefore appears at the beginning, at the end, or in between.

A *noun* is a composite sound with a meaning. It does not indicate time, and no part of it has intrinsic meaning of its own. In compound nouns we do not separately register the meaning of each part of the compound: for example, in the name Theodoros, we do not hear the word *doron* ('gift') in the second half.

A *verb* is a composite sound with a meaning. As with nouns, no part of it has intrinsic meaning of its own. A verb indicates time. 'Man' [a noun] and 'white' [an adjective] do not indicate time, but 'walk' and 'walked' [both parts of the same verb] do indicate time.

An *inflexion* is a modification of a noun or verb [in Greek] to indicate such things as case ('this man's' or 'to this man', for example [in Greek, each is a single word]), number ('man' or 'men', for example [again, each a single word]) or way of speaking ('Walk!' and 'Did he walk?' are verb-inflexions of this kind).

An *utterance* is a composite sound which itself has meaning and whose individual components also have meaning. Not every phrase contains nouns and verbs: the definition 'human being' is an example [neither of its components is a noun or a verb]. An utterance need not contain a verb, but it must always have components with individual meaning, for example 'Kreon' in 'Kreon is walking'. An utterance can be single in two ways: either it means one single thing (eg 'The *Iliad*') or is a group of components with a single composite meaning (eg the the phrase 'human being').

(21) [Translator's note: this section deals elliptically and cryptically with difficult matters, and scribes down the years have tried to make it clearer, with the result that the surviving text is in places gibberish. Scholars have cudgelled their brains to make sense of it, and to relate it to modern understanding of language, and of the Greek language; their success has been mixed. The last paragraph of this section, for example, seems clear enough – but as it stands, it is, quite simply, wrong.]

Words are of two kinds, simple and compound. By simple I mean those composed of parts which have no individual

meaning, like the [Greek] word *ge* ['earth']. By compound
I mean those made up either of one part with individual
meaning and one without (even when the part with meaning
sheds it in the compound), or of parts each of which has
individual meaning. Compound nouns can have three, four
or more component parts: an example is the word 'Hermo-
kaiko-xanthos' [the name of a god, formed from three river-
names].

Every word is either in current use, rare, metaphorical,
ornamental, newly coined, lengthened, contracted or altered.
By 'in current use' I mean used by many people; by 'rare' I
mean used by a few. The same noun can therefore be both 'in
current use' and 'rare', in different areas. The word *sigunon* is
current in Cyprus for 'spear', for example, but rare in Athens.

Metaphor is the transfer of a word from one set of circumstances to another. Metaphors may involve transfer from
genus to species, from species to genus, from species to
species or by analogy. An example of transfer from genus to
species is the sentence 'There lies my ship'; for lying at anchor
is a species of lying. An example of transfer from species to
genus is the sentence [in Homer's *Odyssey*] 'Odysseus has
done ten thousand noble deeds'; for ten thousand is a species
of large number, and is here used for a large number generally.
Examples of transfer from species to species [also from
Homer] are the phrases 'Drawing away the life' and 'Cutting
the water'; both phrases mean 'taking away', and 'drawing
away' stands for 'cutting' and 'cutting' for 'drawing away'.
Metaphor by analogy is as follows. Take four expressions.
When B is to A as D is to C, the author can use B instead of
A and D instead of C. For example: a drinking-cup is to
Dionysos [god of wine] what a shield is to Ares [god of war],
so an author may call a cup 'Dionysos' shield' and a shield
'Ares' cup'. Old age is to life as evening is to day. So we can
call evening 'the day's old age' and old age 'the evening of
life', or, as Empedokles put it, 'life's setting sun'. Sometimes
no words exist for parts of the analogy, but it can still be
made. For example, scattering seed is called sowing, but there
is no specific word for the Sun's scattering of its rays, which
is an analogous process. None the less, an author can [talk of]
'sowing God's fire'. In another way of using this kind of
metaphor, we can use a transferred term and then deny that
term one of its proper attributes, for example calling a shield
not 'Ares' cup' but 'the cup that has no wine'.

An ornamental noun... [text missing]

A newly coined word is one which has never been used before but is invented by the writer. Examples are 'sprouters' for horns [author unknown] and 'supplicator' for priest [in Homer].

A word is lengthened when its usual syllable is replaced by a longer one or extra sounds are inserted. A word is contracted when some part of it is removed. Examples of lengthening are *polehs* for *poleoh* ['of a city'; in Homer; lengthened to fit the verse-metre] and *Peeleeiadeoh* for *Peeleidoo* ['of Peleus' son', ie 'of Achilles'; also Homeric]. Examples of contracted words are *kri* for *krithee* ['barley'; Homeric], *doh* for *doha* ['house'; Homeric] and 'one *ops* ['appearance'] made from two' [Empedokles, perhaps referring to a devoted couple, or to some hybrid creature].

A word is altered when part of the usual form is left unchanged, and the rest is changed. An example is [when Homer, for metrical reasons] writes *dexiteron kata mazdon* ['by the right nipple'], replacing the standard *dexion* with *dexiteron*.

Nouns [in Greek] are masculine, feminine or neuter. Nouns which end in 'n', 'r' and 's' (as well as the two diphthongs involving 's', namely 'ps' and 'ks') are masculine, and nouns which end in long vowels (such as 'ee' or 'oh') and length-ened forms of short vowels (for example long 'a') are feminine – a similar number. No nouns end in mute sounds or short vowels. Only three nouns end in 'i': *meli* ['honey'], *kommi* ['gum'] and *peperi* ['pepper']. Only five nouns end in 'u', and they, as well as nouns ending in 'n' and 's', are neuter. (22) The best style of language is clear without being prosaic. [Obviously,] a style entirely made up of everyday words and expressions will be clear, but it will also be prosaic – as in the work of Kleophon or Sthenelos. A style which is characterful and not prosaic will contain unusual expressions, unfamiliar words, metaphors, words which are lengthened – none of it, in short, will be everyday. But if it consists of nothing but such words and expressions it will be either riddling or gibberish: riddling if it uses metaphors, gibberish if it uses unfamiliar words. Riddles describe reality in fanciful ways, something which is impossible with everyday words but easy with metaphor: as in the famous riddle [describing someone 'cupping' someone else, holding a bronze bowl to a small cut in the skin and then heating it to create a vacuum and draw out infected blood] 'I watched a man on another man glue bronze by fire'. Gibberish consists of bizarre or unusual words. We should use such things, but use them judiciously.

Unusual words, metaphors and poetic expressions will
elevate our style, while everyday words will keep it accessible.

[In Greek,] an excellent way to produce language which is
both elevated and accessible is to lengthen, shorten or change
[certain] words. Because the words are changed from their
everyday forms, they will add distinction; because they are
close enough to their everyday forms, they will be
comprehensible. Some critics quite wrongly pillory this
process and the authors who use it. Eukleides the elder said
roundly that being a poet was easy if all you had to do was
fiddle around with the lengths of words. He wrote two
parodies to prove his point: 'Awalking all adown the road I
see-see-see a chappie' and 'He wouldn't take his medicine, he
spitty-spat it out'. Obviously, if you go that far you are
producing jokes not poetry – as you would be if you overdid
metaphors, unusual words or any other stylistic ingredients.
[Homer's] epics show how lengthening should be done, and
the difference it makes can be seen if you simply replace the
lengthened words with their more everyday equivalents.

It is the same with the other effects. For example,
Euripides once used a line of verse already used by
Aeschylus – and by changing a single word, made it
seem stylish rather than prosaic. Aeschylus wrote, in his
Philoktetes [now lost], 'This ulcer eats my foot';
Euripides wrote 'This ulcer feasts on my foot'.

Other examples [from works now lost, by authors unknown]
are 'I that am weakly and of no account' instead of the prosaic
'I'm weak and useless', 'A crooked stool he fetched, and a
table barely broad' instead of 'He fetched a cheap stool and a
small table' or 'The sea-shore booms' instead of 'The beach
clears its throat'. [Translator's note: the point is much more
powerful in the Greek lines Aristotle parodies. In English,
one might get a similar effect by replacing Shakespeare's
'Night's candles are burnt out, and jocund day/Stands tiptoe
on the misty mountaintops', from *Romeo and Juliet*, with
something like 'The stars have gone in, and it'll soon be
dawn'.]

On a similar note, when Ariphrades mocked dramatists
for writing things no one would ever say (for example
'from the palace out he comes' instead of 'he's coming
out of the palace'), he completely missed the point that
it is precisely because such changes are *not* the sort of

things anyone would ever say in ordinary life that they give the style distinction.

So: all stylistic devices (unusual or compound words) should be used carefully and exactly. Metaphor is the most important tool of all. No one can really teach it, since looking at one thing and seeing another is a natural, inborn gift.

So far as the various kinds of words [in Greek] are concerned, dithyrambs are best suited to compound words, epic to one using unusual words, iambics [the bulk of the spoken parts of drama] to one using metaphor. Epic, of course, can use them all. But iambics generally represent ordinary speech, and the most appropriate stylistic ingredients are therefore those we might use in ordinary speech: everyday words, metaphor and expressions which give [emotional] colouring.

I turn now from tragedy (the art of representing real life by stage action) to other forms of imitation.

Epic

(23) Epic is the imitation of events in verse by narrative without action. Its *muthos*, like that of tragedy, should be constructed on dramatic principles. It should satisfy because of its own organic unity, as if it were a living creature, and to that end its subject should be single, whole and complete, and it should have a beginning, a middle and an end. Its structure will differ from that of history, which deals, by definition, not with a single subject but a single period, and must include everything that happened in that period to individuals and groups of people, whether or not the events are connected. In the sequence of events things follow one another without connection. Sea battles were fought in the same year [480BC] at Salamis [against the Persians] and in Sicily against the Carthaginians, but they are otherwise not connected.

It has to be said that most writers understand this. It is yet another of the areas in which Homer betters all others. The Trojan War had a clear beginning and end, and yet he makes no attempt to cover its entirety [in the *Iliad*]: it would be too long, or if he kept it short, too complicated. Accordingly, he deals with just part of it, creating variety by referring in passing to events outside his main narrative (for example in the Catalogue of Ships). Other writers of epic, who centre on single heroes, single periods or single stretches of action, offer too many plot-strands.

Examples are the *Cypria* and the *Minor Iliad* [both now lost; authors unknown; the *Cypria* dealt with events leading up to the Trojan War and the *Minor Iliad* with the Fall of Troy, events following on Homer's *Iliad*]. The result is that whereas only single tragedies could be made from the *Iliad* or the *Odyssey*, the *Cypria* offers plots for several and the *Minor Iliad* material for at least eight – the judgement about Achilles' armour, the stories of Philoktetes, Neoptolemos and Eurypylos, Odysseus as a beggar, the story of the Laconian women, the fall of Troy, the departure of the fleet – not to mention the stories of Sinon and the women of Troy.

(24) Like tragedy [see chapters 10, 18], epic should be 'simple' or 'complex', should be based on character or suffering. With the exceptions of lyricism and spectacle, its components should also be the same; it should contain reversals, discoveries and scenes of mourning, and its thought and language should be elevated. Homer's work, once again, offers the earliest and finest examples of all these. His epics are differently structured: the *Iliad* has a 'simple' plot and is based on suffering, the *Odyssey* is 'complex' (full of discovery scenes) and is based on character. In each of them, the poetry and the thought are outstanding.

Epic differs from tragedy in length and metre. In an earlier section [chapter 7], I suggested that the appropriate length meant embracing the whole thing, from beginning to end, in a single experience: that is, not the length of the old epics but of the group of four plays performed on a single festival day. [Four plays together contain 5000-6000 lines of verse; the *Iliad* and *Odyssey* are each three times as long.] Epic, however, has the potential – the unique potential – to be longer. **Tragedy is unable to represent several different events happening at the same time; it has to restrict itself to what the actors are performing at any single moment.** By contrast, the narrative form of epic allows events which happen simultaneously to be presented together – and if they are relevant to one another, they add richness and variety to the whole. This both gives epic its grandeur and keeps its listeners intrigued and entertained. People are bored by lack of variety – a fact which has been the downfall of many a tragedy.

Experience has shown that hexameters are the best metre for epic. Another metre, or a variety of metres, would not work so well. Hexameters are the grandest and stateliest of all metres, fit for the unusual words and metaphors which give epic its unique quality. Iambics and trochaics are fast-moving, lively metres, iambics ideal for natural-seeming conversation and trochaics excellent for dancing. The epics of Chairemon show the folly of trying to write in a variety of metres. Hexameters are the ideal form for epic poems: Nature itself has laid down this law.

Another aspect in which Homer is to be admired is his sure sense of how much to use the first person in his work. Authors should use the first person as seldom as possible: this is not the function of *mimesis*. Some writers are forever striding into their own compositions, allowing little scope for creation. Homer has a brief introduction, then immediately introduces a man, a woman or some other person – and he always gives them character.

Epic offers even more scope than tragedy for that essential ingredient [of imitation], the larger than life. This is because, instead of seeing amazing events performed by actors, we hear them described. The scene where Achilles chases Hektor [three times round the walls of Troy] would be ludicrous on the stage: the Greeks standing like dummies and Achilles shaking his head to stop them joining in. In epic such elements of absurdity pass unnoticed. Everyone takes pleasure in the

larger than life – you have only to hear someone telling
an anecdote to realise that. Homer shows how it should
be done: by [the rhetorical trick known as] false
inference. If A leads to B, people infer that because
B is the case, A must also be the case. This is not so.
B can be the case and follow from A even if A is false –
as happens in the bath scene in the *Odyssey*.

[The scene contains two false inferences. First Odysseus,
disguised as a stranger from Crete, tells Penelope that he
knows Odysseus and describes his clothes, and Penelope
begins with idea A (that if the stranger's story were true he
would know the details he describes), moves to idea B (that
he *does* know the details) and falsely infers that because he
knows the details the story must be true. Later, the old nurse
Eurykleia, washing the stranger in his bath, begins with idea
A (that the stranger has a scar), moves to idea B (that
Odysseus had a scar) and moves to the inference that the
stranger is Odysseus. Homer makes ironical use of this
second example: Odysseus tells Eurykleia that she is
mistaken, and we (the audience) know that she has in fact hit
on the truth.]

Writers should always prefer things which are
impossible but convincing to incidents which are
possible but unconvincing. Plots should be plausible,
and if implausible elements are unavoidable, they
should be kept out of the main action (like Oedipus'
ignorance of how his father died in Sophocles' *Oedipus
Tyrannos*), rather than be made essential to the plot, like
the (false) story of Orestes' death at the Pythian Games
in Euripides' *Elektra* or the fact that Telephos was able
to go all the way from Tegeia to Mysia without once
speaking. It is no defence to say that the *muthos* would
be ruined without such elements. They should never be
there in the first place, and if there are better ways of
organising the *muthos*, and an author chooses to ignore
them, that author is not just a bad writer but a fool.
Even in the *Odyssey* the scene where Odysseus is put
ashore in Ithaka while still asleep would be ridiculous in
the hands of a lesser writer. Homer, the master, veils
implausibility in sheer poetic charm.

Elevated language should be reserved for passages
where the action slows down, where there is no display
of character or argument. If a scene depends on character or argument, flashy language will obscure it.

Criticism and How to Respond to It

(25) I turn to the way people deal with 'problem
passages'. I begin with four assertions about literary
creation. (a) Authors, like painters and sculptors, make
imitations of three kinds: of things as they are or used
to be, things as people say or think they are, and things
as they ought to be. (b) Authors create these imitations
by the use of language: current words, rare words,
metaphors and other professional techniques. (c)
Imaginative writing, like any of the arts, has different
criteria of 'correctness' from those in everyday life.
(d) Artistic 'errors' are of two kinds, inherent and
incidental. If someone tries to represent something but
lacks the technique to do it properly, this is inherent
error. If, however, a mistake is made in detail – for
example when [a painter] shows a galloping horse with
both front legs off the ground at the same time, or gets
wrong some technicality in, say, medicine – the error is
[incidental and] not inherent.

These points should be borne in mind in any discussion
of literary criticism.

Let us begin with criticisms of technical competence.
If an author describes something which is impossible,
this is an 'error', but it is justified if it works: that is, as
I have said above, if it makes part of the work, or the
whole work, more effective. [Homer's description of]
Achilles chasing Hektor is a case in point. But if the
effect could have been made without breaking the rules,
the error is not justified. One must also ask whether the
error is intrinsic or incidental. It is less important, for
example, to know that a female deer has no horns than
to paint it badly.

An author, accused of not imitating reality, can always
answer, 'This is reality as it ought to be' – as Sophocles
said, contrasting Euripides' characters ('people as they
are') with his own ('people as they ought to be'). If
neither is the case, if things depicted are neither reality
nor idealised reality, a third explanation might be that
they conform with general belief. Depictions of gods
are an example.

Xenophanes [a philosopher who objected to gods being
shown in human form] may be right, and the ways gods are
shown is neither accurate nor appropriate, but they do follow
tradition.

One can also say that what an author shows or describes
may not be true now, but was so once.

Homer talks of soldiers 'sticking their spearbutts in the
ground'. No one except the Illyrians does that nowadays, but
it was done (Homer might claim) in the days of Troy.

When one comes on to moral truth, the issue must be
decided not in terms of the absolute moral 'goodness'
or 'badness' of each action, but also of who does it, to
whom, how and why (for example to avoid a greater
'wrong' or bring about a greater 'right').

Some criticisms may be countered by pleading 'poetic
licence'.

A word may be unusual, for example *oureeas* in the *Iliad* line
where 'Apollo first attacked the mules' – perhaps it means
'watchmen' not 'mules'. 'Dolon the cripple ran fast' may
actually be 'Dolon the ugly ran fast' – in Cretan [Greek] the
same word is used for both. 'Mix the wine stronger' may not
mean to make it suitable for drunks, but 'mix it harder'. Other
phrases may be metaphorical, for example 'All the gods slept,
but Zeus was waking,' or 'All the heroes slept, but Agamemnon
was waking': 'all' is simply standing for 'most'. Similarly, 'she
alone did not share' [when in fact none of her sisters shared
either] may be simply a way of saying 'She in particular,
standing out from the others, did not share... '

In other passages, strange-seeming expressions can be
changed, as [the grammarian] Hippias of Thasos pointed out,
by changing the accent on a word [which often materially

changes its meaning], or by repunctuating. Other oddities are explainable by custom: just as we say 'wine' when we mean 'wine-and-water', so Homer may say 'leg-armour made of tin' when he means [the standard] 'leg-armour made of tin-and-copper alloy' [ie bronze]. Iron-workers are regularly called 'bronze-smiths', and Ganymede, cup-bearer of the gods, is often called 'the gods' wine-steward'. Admittedly, these last examples could be metaphors.

Wherever the meaning of a phrase seems peculiar, we should consider its context.

For example, when Homer [talking of Aeneas' spear piercing the five layers of Achilles' god-made shield, two layers of gold, two of bronze and one of tin,] says 'it pierced right through, though it was checked by the gold', we have to ask precisely what he meant by 'checked'. This is the exact opposite of the suggestion by Glaukon, that people make unreasonable assumptions, then base their criticisms on those rather than what the author actually wrote. The case of Ikarios [father of Odysseus' wife Penelope] is typical. People assume that he was from Sparta, and find it strange, therefore, that when Telemachos visits Sparta he never meets him. The Kephallenians however say that Penelope's father came from their area, and that his name was not Ikarios but Ikadios. [In short,] the critical quibble [about Telemachos] may be based on a mistake.

To sum up:

(a) The impossible must be justified by reference to artistic requirements, to the higher reality or to tradition. In artistic matters, what is plausible but impossible is preferable to what is possible but implausible. It may well be impossible for any real person to be like those painted by Zeuxis. 'Yes,' we might argue, 'And more's the pity, since his idealised people far surpass reality.'

(b) Popular tradition may be used to defend what seems to defy reason. Sometimes they are not unreasonable anyway, since it is reasonable to assume that the unreasonable could happen.

(c) Contradictions should be examined as carefully as your opponent's arguments in a discussion. Is the author utterly consistent, always saying the same thing in the same way? Or are there contradictions, either between what he or she said before or between the claimed meaning of the words and the meaning any intelligent person might give to them?

(d) If improbabilities in the plot and 'badness' of character are unnecessary and no good dramatic use is made of them, it is reasonable to criticise them. Aigeus' arrival in Euripides' *Medea* is unnecessary. In Euripides' *Orestes* there is no need for the 'badness' of Menelaos' character.

Critical objections are on five main grounds: that things are impossible, unlikely, harmful, contradictory or against the rules of the art. There are, as I have outlined above, twelve answers. [1. 'That's how things were.' 2. 'That's how things are.' 3. 'That's how things are traditionally said to be.' 4. 'That's how things seem.' 5. 'That's how things should be.' 6. 'The word used is rare.' 7. 'It's a metaphor.' 8. 'The accent is wrong.' 9. 'The punctuation is wrong.' 10. 'The word's ambiguous.' 11. 'The odd word or phrase is common everyday speech.' 12. 'Artistic licence.']

Comparison of Epic and Tragedy

26. The question is sometimes asked whether epic or tragedy is the superior form of imitation. If by 'superior' we mean less common and by 'less common' we mean the one which appeals to people of refinement, then an art which imitates anything and everything is plainly vulgar. Audiences are thought to be too stupid to follow them unless the performers put in their own contribution, rushing hither and thither, the musicians whirling round as if they were throwing the discus or pulling the chorus-leader about as if [he were Odysseus and] they were [the sea-monster] Skylla. Tragedy has become what the older generation of actors used to complain of in their juniors. Mynisskos [one of Aeschylus' company]

called Kallippides [who acted a generation later, among
others for Aristophanes] 'the great ape' because of his
over-acting, and similar remarks were made about
Pindaros. Tragedy is to epic what those younger actors
are to their elders. Epic is for a cultured audience who
need no acting-out; tragedy is for a less discriminating
public – and since it is popular, it must be inferior.

These criticisms are to do with acting, not with forms
of literature. A bard reciting epic, or a solo singer in a
dithyramb, can wave his arms about just as much as a
stage actor: remember Sosistratos, not to mention
Mnasitheus from Opous. Not all physical acting or
dancing is to be condemned, only that of performers
who play low-class people: Kallippides, for example,
or the actors of today who specialise in playing
uncontrolled women. [Translator's note: Playing
emotion-racked women was, in fact, a highly-skilled art,
practised from earliest times, and given scope by such
parts as Kassandra in Aeschylus' *Agamemnon*, Io in his
Prometheus, Sophocles' Elektra and many of Euripides'
finest surviving creations, from Medea to Kreousa, from
Hecuba to Phaidra.] Not only that, but tragedy, like
epic, can make its effect without stage action, merely
by being read. Excess of action is not a fault inherent
in the genre.

Secondly, tragedy is superior because it uses all the
components of epic – even hexameters are possible –
and adds crucial extra pleasure by means of its own
particular elements, music and spectacle. This vividness,
too, is as much apparent when it is read as when it is
acted. It achieves its purpose far more economically,
giving a concentrated effect rather than one spread
over a long stretch of time. Imagine *Oedipus Tyrannos*
stretched to the length of the *Iliad*! Epic depends far less
on unity: one epic will provide plots for a dozen
tragedies. If an epic poet does write a single *muthos*, it
either foreshortens the form or is stretched to fit it and
so diluted. When I say that 'epic depends far less on
unity' I mean that each poem incorporates several

stories, each with density of their own. The *Iliad* and *Odyssey* are examples of this, and yet each is so artfully constructed that it is, to the highest extent the form permits, the imitation of a single action [see chapter 1].

If tragedy surpasses epic in these respects, and also fulfils its artistic function more perfectly – not any artistic function, but the one I have outlined [throughout this book: see especially chapter 14], it follows that it is the superior artform.

Conclusion

So much for tragedy and epic, in general and in particular, together with discussion of their component elements, the differences between them, the reasons why authors succeed or fail, the kind of objections critics raise and the way they can be answered.

[Translator's note: *Poetics* ends here. A few sentences survive which appear to be parts of a similar treatise on comedy, but it seems to be a separate book (or lecture).]

Key Dates

NB all are BC

Before 700	Homer
c532	First 'tragedy' performed in Athens
c525	Aeschylus born
496	Sophocles born
485/480	Euripides born
480	Greeks destroy Persian fleet at battle of Salamis
472	Aeschylus' *Persians*
c469	Socrates born
458	Aeschylus' *Oresteia*
456	Aeschylus died
c445	Aristophanes born
441	Sophocles' *Antigone*
431	Euripides' *Medea*; Peloponnesian War begins between Athens, Sparta and their respective allies
c429	Sophocles' *Oedipus Tyrannos*; Plato born
428	Euripides' *Hippolytos*
415	Euripides' *Women of Troy*
c414	Euripides' *Iphigeneia in Tauris*
413	Euripides' *Elektra*
411	Aristophanes' *Lysistrata*
406	Euripides and Sophocles died
405	Aristophanes' *Frogs*
404	Athens defeated in Peloponnesian War
399	Socrates executed
c385	Aristophanes died
384	Aristotle born
c375	Plato's *Republic*
347	Plato died
c345	Aristotle's *Poetics*
322	Aristotle died

Who's Who

NB all dates are BC

Aeschylus (c525-456). Athenian writer of tragedies. Seven survive, including the *Oresteia* trilogy.

Agathon (c447-401). Athenian writer of tragedies. None survive.

Alkibiades (fifth century). Controversial Athenian soldier and politician.

Ariphrades (late fifth century). Athenian literary/dramatic figure, mocked by Aristophanes.

Aristophanes (c445-c385). Athenian writer of comedy. Eleven plays survive, including *Lysistrata* and *Birds*.

Astydamas (fourth century). Two writers of tragedy had this name, father and son. No plays survive.

Chairemon (4th century). Athenian writer of tragedy. His style was apparently florid and artificial. No plays survive.

Chionides (early fifth century). Athenian writer of comedy, perhaps winner of the first Athenian competition in 487. Nothing survives.

Dikaiogenes (late fifth century). Writer of tragedy. No plays survive.

Dionysios (fifth century). Painter and/or sculptor. Nothing known.

Epicharmos (late sixth century). Sicilian writer of comedies, one of the earliest. Nothing survives.

Empedokles (fifth century). Sicilian scientist and philosopher.

Eukleides (late fifth century). Megarian philosopher.

Euripides (485/480-406). Athenian writer of tragedy. Nineteen plays survive, including *Medea*, *Iphigeneia in Tauris*, *Women of Troy* and *Bacchae*

Glaukon (date unknown). Nothing definite known.

Hegemon (fifth century).Writer of parodies. Nothing survives.

Herodotos (c484-420). Writer from Halikarnassos, the first historian.

Homer (perhaps eighth century). Writer of epic poems. Main surviving works are the *Iliad* and *Odyssey*.

Kallippides (late fifth century). Actor from Euripides' time.

Karkinos (fourth century). Athenian writer of tragedy, grandson of another Karkinos, also a playwright. Nothing survives.

Kleophon (fourth century). Perhaps Athenian writer. Nothing known.

Hippias (date unknown). Grammarian from Thasos. Nothing known.

Magnes (fifth century). Athenian writer of comedy, one of the earliest. No plays survive.

Mnasitheus (early fourth century). Flamboyant solo performer.

Mynniskos (early fifth century). Actor from Aeschylus' time.

Nichochares (fourth century). Athenian writer of satire. None survives.

Pauson. Fine artist. Nothing known.

Philoxenos (early fourth century). Cytheran poet, active in Sicily. Nothing survives.

Phormis (early fifth century). Sicilian writer of comedy. Nothing survives.

Pindar (early fifth century). Theban poet, known especially for choruses and solo songs. Ceremonial and celebratory odes survive.

Polyeidos (date unknown). Philosopher, perhaps also writer of tragedy. Nothing known.

Polygnotos (fifth century). Athenian painter and sculptor, famous in his day for the 'classical' elegance of his work. None survives.

Protagoras (c490-420). Philosopher from Abdera, known especially for his theological writings.

Socrates (c469-399). Athenian philosopher, famous for his style of pursuing truth through dialogue, gradually eliminating irrelevant or inaccurate ideas and arguments. Teacher of Plato, who in turn taught Aristotle.

Sophocles (496-406). Athenian writer of tragedies. Seven survive, including *Oedipus Tyrannos* and *Antigone.*

Sophron (fifth century). Sicilian writer of *mimoi* (prose comic sketches). None survive.

Sosistratos (fourth century). Flamboyant solo performer.

Sthenelos (fifth century). Athenian writer of tragedy, known only by references to his incompetence.

Theagenes (seventh century). Megarian dictator.

Theodektes (fourth century). Athenian writer. Poet, philosopher, tragedian, author of works on rhetoric and grammar. Only fragments survive.

Timotheos (late fifth century). Milesian writer of *nomes* (religious songs). Musical pioneer but stilted versifier. Only a handful of lines survive.

Xenarchos (fifth century). Sicilian writer of *mimoi*, son of Sophron. Nothing survives.

Xenophanes (sixth century). Poet and philosopher.

Zeuxis (late fifth century). Sicilian painter renowned for his realism.